PROPAGATING PLANT FOR BEGINNERS

The Essential Guide to Unlock the Secrets of Propagating for Gardeners

Sylvia K. Smith

Copyright © 2023 by [Sylvia K. Smith]

All rights reserved. No part of this book may be reproduced in any form or by any electronic or mechanical means, including information storage and retrieval systems, without permission in writing from the publisher, except by a reviewer who may quote brief passages in a review.

This book is a work of nonfiction. The views expressed herein are the sole responsibility of the author and do not necessarily reflect those of the publisher or its agents.

Table of Contents

Introduction
Chapter 1: Why Propagate Plants?
   Benefits of Propagating Plants
   Terms You Should Know
Chapter 2: Understanding Plant Propagation
   What is Plant Propagation?
   Different Methods of Propagation
   Factors Affecting Plant Propagation
Chapter 3: Essential Tools and Materials
Chapter 4: Propagation by Seeds
   Common Mistakes to avoid
Chapter 5: Propagation by Cuttings
   Types of Cuttings
   Troubleshooting Common Issues in Propagation by Cuttings:
Chapter 6: Propagation by Division
   Tips for Successful Division in Plant Propagation:
Chapter 7: Propagation by Layering
   Types of Layering

Root Development and Separation

Chapter 8: Care and Maintenance of Propagated Plants

Chapter 9: Troubleshooting Common Issues with Propagated Plants

Chapter 10: Propagating Specific Plant Species

Chapter 11: Taking Your Propagation Skills Further

Chapter 12: Advanced Tips and Techniques for Plant Propagation

Conclusion

Introduction

Welcome to "Propagating Plants for Beginners," a comprehensive guide designed to help you embark on your journey of plant propagation. Whether you're an enthusiastic gardener or simply someone looking to expand their plant collection, this guide will provide you with the knowledge and skills needed to propagate plants successfully.

Plant propagation is the process of creating new plants from existing ones, and it offers numerous benefits. By propagating plants, you can multiply your favorite specimens, preserve rare or endangered species, rejuvenate aging plants, and save money by growing your plants from cuttings or seeds instead of purchasing new ones.

Furthermore, the act of propagating plants can be a rewarding and fulfilling experience that deepens your understanding and connection with nature.

Chapter 1: Why Propagate Plants?

Plant propagation is a common activity among horticulturists, gardeners, and other plant lovers due to several compelling reasons. First and foremost, propagation enables the growth and multiplication of plant populations. Gardeners may expand displays, fill voids, or even start new gardens with their preferred species by generating new plants from old ones.

To save plants, proper propagation is equally essential. To protect their genetic variety and stop extinction, many rare or endangered plants are propagated. These priceless plants may be reproduced and returned to their original environments using techniques like seed preservation, cutting propagation, or tissue culture.

Plant propagation has positive economic effects. To accommodate the need for different plant species, commercial nurseries rely on propagation methods, assuring a consistent supply for horticultural projects, home gardening, and landscaping.

Plant propagation also enables people to express their creativity and create novel cultivars. Gardeners may produce one-of-a-kind hybrids by breeding plants together and choosing those with attractive characteristics, adding to the variety and beauty of plant species.

Plant propagation is a gratifying effort for both amateurs and experts since it serves utilitarian, conservational, economic, and creative reasons.

Benefits of Propagating Plants

There are several reasons why plant propagation is a valuable skill for beginners to acquire.

Firstly, it allows you to replicate your favorite plants, ensuring that their unique characteristics and traits are preserved. Whether it's a stunning flower, a delicious fruit-bearing tree, or a vibrant foliage plant, propagating allows you to create multiple copies that can be enjoyed in various locations or shared with friends and family.

Propagating plants can be an environmentally friendly practice. By growing your plants from seeds, cuttings, or divisions, you reduce the demand for commercially produced plants, which often involve intensive farming practices and transportation. This promotes sustainability and helps conserve natural resources.

Moreover, propagation provides an opportunity to experiment and explore your creativity. It allows you to try different techniques, such as grafting or tissue culture, and push the boundaries of what you can achieve as a gardener. It opens doors to hybridization, cross-pollination, and the creation of unique plant varieties.

Terms You Should Know

Before delving into the various methods of plant propagation, it's essential to familiarize yourself with some basic terminology:

I. **Propagation**: The process of creating new plants from existing ones.

II. **Cutting**: A severed piece of a plant, usually a stem or leaf, which can be used to propagate a new plant.

III. **Division**: The separation of an established plant into smaller sections, each capable of growing independently.

IV. **Layering**: A method of propagation where a stem or branch is encouraged to produce roots while still attached to the parent plant, before being separated to form a new plant.

V. **Grafting**: Joining the tissues of two different plants to create a single plant with desirable characteristics from both parent plants.

VI. **Budding**: Inserting a bud from one plant into the stem or bark of another plant to allow it to grow and develop.

VII. **Tissue Culture**: A laboratory-based technique for propagating plants using small tissue samples and nutrient media under sterile conditions.

Now that we have covered the basics, let's explore the world of plant propagation together and equip you with the knowledge and skills to become a successful propagator.

Chapter 2: Understanding Plant Propagation

What is Plant Propagation?

Plant propagation is the art and science of creating new plants from existing ones. It involves various techniques and methods to reproduce plants, allowing gardeners, horticulturists, and plant enthusiasts to expand their collections, preserve unique plant varieties, and propagate rare or endangered species.

In nature, plants reproduce through sexual and asexual means. Sexual reproduction occurs through the exchange of pollen between male and female flower parts, leading to the production of seeds. Asexual reproduction, on the other hand, involves the generation of new plants without the involvement of seeds or fertilization.

Plant propagation methods exploit the natural ability of plants to regenerate and produce new shoots, roots, or whole plants from different plant parts, such as seeds, stems, leaves, roots, or specialized structures. These methods allow gardeners to reproduce plants with desirable characteristics, including specific flower colors, fruit flavors, disease resistance, or growth habits.

Different Methods of Propagation

There are several primary methods of plant propagation, each suitable for different plant species and conditions. Let's explore some of the commonly used methods:

Seed Propagation:

Seed propagation involves collecting and germinating seeds to grow new plants. It is a simple and widely accessible method. Seeds can be obtained from mature plants, purchased from nurseries, or acquired through seed exchanges. This method is commonly used for annuals, biennials, and some perennials.

Cutting Propagation:

Cutting propagation involves taking a section of a plant, typically a stem or a leaf, and encouraging it to develop roots and grow into a new plant. This method allows for the replication of plant traits and is used for a wide range of plants, including herbaceous perennials, woody shrubs, and vines.

Division Propagation:

Division propagation involves dividing a mature plant into smaller sections, each containing roots and shoots. This method is suitable for plants with clumping or rhizomatous growth habits, such as ornamental grasses, hostas, and many perennials. Divisions are replanted, and each section grows into a new plant.

Layering Propagation:

Layering propagation encourages a stem or branch of a plant to produce roots while still attached to the parent plant. Once the roots develop, the layered section can be separated and planted as an independent plant. This method is often used for plants with flexible branches, such as certain shrubs, climbers, and fruit trees.

Grafting and Budding:

Grafting and budding are advanced techniques that involve joining the tissues of two different plants to create a single plant with desirable traits. Grafting involves joining a stem or a branch (scion) from one plant onto the rootstock of another compatible plant. Budding is a similar technique but involves inserting a bud instead of a stem. Grafting and budding are commonly used in fruit tree production, rose cultivation, and creating unique plant varieties.

Tissue Culture Propagation:

Tissue culture propagation, also known as micropropagation, is a laboratory-based method that involves growing plants from tiny tissue samples under sterile conditions. This technique allows for the rapid multiplication of plants and the production of disease-free specimens. Tissue culture is often used for rare or valuable plant species, orchids, and improving crops.

Factors Affecting Plant Propagation

Successful plant propagation relies on understanding and managing various factors that influence the growth and development of plants. These factors include:

Light and Temperature:

Different plants have varying light and temperature requirements. Understanding the optimal light levels and temperature ranges for each plant species is crucial for successful propagation. Some plants thrive in full sun, while others prefer shade or specific temperature conditions.

Humidity and Moisture:

Proper humidity and moisture levels are essential for successful plant propagation. Some plants prefer high humidity, while others require drier conditions. Balancing moisture levels is crucial to prevent rot or dehydration during the propagation process.

Soil and Nutrients:

Selecting the appropriate soil or growing medium for each plant species is vital. Some plants require well-draining soil, while others thrive in moisture-retentive media. Providing the necessary nutrients, such as fertilizers or organic matter, ensures optimal growth and development of propagated plants.

Timing and Seasonality:

Timing plays a crucial role in plant propagation. Understanding the specific season or stage of growth when a plant is most receptive to propagation is essential for success. Some plants root more easily during spring or early summer, while others require specific dormancy periods or specific environmental cues.

Pruning and Maintenance:

Pruning techniques and plant maintenance practices can greatly influence the success of plant propagation. Proper pruning can stimulate new growth and provide suitable cutting material, while regular care, such as watering, fertilizing, and pest control, ensures healthy parent plants and the viability of propagated specimens.

By understanding the various methods of plant propagation and the factors that influence successful propagation, you will be well-equipped to embark on your journey as a plant propagator.

Chapter 3: Essential Tools and Materials

To embark on your plant propagation journey, it's important to have the right tools and materials at your disposal. Here are some essential items you'll need:

Choosing the Right Tools:

- **Pruning Shears:** Sharp and sturdy pruning shears are essential for taking clean and precise cuttings from plants. Look for bypass pruners, which have a scissor-like cutting action, for clean cuts that promote successful rooting.

- **Garden Knife:** A sharp, clean garden knife is useful for taking specific types of cuttings and preparing plant material for propagation. It can also be used for making clean cuts during grafting or budding.

- **Rooting Hormone:** Rooting hormone is a powdered or liquid substance that promotes the formation of roots on cuttings. It's especially useful for difficult-to-root plants. Look for a rooting hormone product specifically designed for plant propagation.

- **Labels and Markers:** Keeping track of your plant varieties is essential. Use labels and markers to identify the different plants, propagation methods, and dates. This will help you monitor their progress and make adjustments if needed.

- **Mist Sprayer or Spray Bottle:** A mist sprayer or spray bottle filled with water is useful for maintaining proper humidity levels when propagating plants. Mist the cuttings or newly planted specimens to keep them moist without causing waterlogged conditions.

- **Seed Trays or Pots:** Seed trays or pots provide suitable containers for starting seeds or rooting cuttings. Opt for trays with drainage holes or use individual pots to ensure proper moisture balance.

- **Propagation Medium:** Choose a suitable medium based on the plant species and propagation method. This could include a seed-starting mix, sterile potting soil, vermiculite, perlite, or a specialized rooting medium.

- **Propagation Dome or Plastic Bag:** A propagation dome or plastic bag can be used to create a mini greenhouse effect, providing a controlled environment for rooting cuttings or germinating seeds. This helps maintain high humidity and prevents excessive moisture loss.

Sterilization Techniques:

Sterilization is essential to prevent the spread of diseases and ensure the success of your plant propagation endeavors. Here are some sterilization techniques:

- **Cleaning Tools:** Before each use, clean your pruning shears, garden knife, and other tools with a solution of 1 part bleach to 9 parts water or rubbing alcohol. This helps eliminate any potential pathogens.

- **Sterilizing Growing Medium:** If reusing pots, trays, or propagation containers, wash them thoroughly with hot, soapy water, and rinse well. You can also sterilize them by soaking them in a solution of 1 part bleach to 9 parts water, followed by rinsing and drying.

Necessary Containers and Mediums:

Choose the appropriate containers and mediums based on the specific propagation method:

- **Seed Trays or Pots:** Use shallow seed trays with drainage holes or small individual pots for starting seeds. Ensure they are clean and sterilized.

- **Propagation Medium:** Depending on the method, use a suitable propagation medium such as a well-draining seed-starting mix, sterile potting soil, or a specialized rooting medium. The medium should provide good aeration and moisture retention while allowing for root development.

Additional Equipment for Specific Propagation Methods:

Certain propagation methods may require additional equipment or materials:

- **Heat Mat:** A heat mat provides bottom heat, promoting root growth and germination in seeds and cuttings that prefer warmer conditions.

- **Grow Lights:** If propagating indoors or in low-light conditions, supplementary grow lights can ensure adequate light levels for healthy growth.

- **Grafting Tape or Rubber Bands:** Grafting and budding require materials to secure the joined plant parts. Grafting tape or rubber bands are commonly used to hold the scion and rootstock together until they unite.

Chapter 4: Propagation by Seeds

Propagating plants by seeds is an exciting and rewarding method that allows you to grow a wide variety of plants. It's a cost-effective way to expand your garden and explore new plant species. Here's a step-by-step guide on how to propagate plants by seeds:

Selecting and Collecting Seeds:
- **Choose Seeds**: Decide on the plant species you want to propagate and obtain seeds. You can collect seeds from mature plants in your garden, purchase them from reputable seed suppliers, or participate in seed exchanges with fellow gardeners.

- **Seed Maturity**: Ensure that the seeds you collect are fully matured. This is indicated by changes in color, firmness, or drying of seed pods or fruits. For purchased seeds, check the packaging for information on seed maturity.

- **Seed Viability**: Determine seed viability by performing a germination test. Place a few seeds on a damp paper towel, seal them in a plastic bag, and keep them in a warm location. After a specified period, check how many seeds have sprouted. Higher sprouting rates indicate higher seed viability.

Seed Preparation:
- **Seed Cleaning**: Remove any debris, chaff, or non-seed material from the collected seeds. You can do this by hand-picking or using sieves to separate the seeds from unwanted particles.

- **Seed Soaking (Optional):** Some seeds benefit from soaking before sowing. This can help break seed dormancy or improve germination rates. Research the specific plant species you are propagating to determine if soaking is necessary and the appropriate duration.

Sowing Seeds:

Choose Containers: Select seed trays, pots, or seed-starting trays with drainage holes. Ensure they are clean and sterilized to prevent disease and fungal issues.

Seed-Starting Mix: Fill the containers with a well-draining seed-starting mix. This should be a sterile medium that provides good aeration and moisture retention. Avoid using garden soil, as it may contain pests or diseases.

Sowing Depth: Check the seed packet or research the specific plant species for the recommended sowing depth. Generally, small seeds are sown shallowly, while larger seeds can be planted deeper.

Sow Seeds: Place the seeds on the prepared soil surface, following the recommended spacing provided for each plant species. Gently press them into the soil or cover them lightly with a thin layer of the seed-starting mix.

Watering: Moisten the soil gently after sowing to ensure good seed-to-soil contact. Use a mist sprayer or a watering can with a fine nozzle to avoid displacing the seeds. Maintain proper moisture levels throughout the germination period.

Germination and Seedling Care:

Location and Temperature: Place the seed trays in a warm and well-lit location. Most seeds germinate best at temperatures between 65°F (18°C) and 75°F (24°C). Provide adequate ventilation to prevent fungal diseases.

Light Requirements: Some seeds require light for germination, while others need darkness. Refer to the specific plant species or seed packet for light requirements. Adjust lighting conditions accordingly.

Germination Period: Different plant species have varying germination times. Some seeds may germinate quickly, while others may take weeks or even months. Patience is key during this period.

Thinning Seedlings: Once the seedlings have emerged and developed their first set of true leaves, thin them out if they are overcrowded. Remove weaker seedlings, leaving only the healthiest and strongest ones.

Watering: Water the seedlings regularly, keeping the soil moist but not waterlogged. Use a watering can or mist sprayer to avoid damaging delicate seedlings. Adjust the watering frequency based on the moisture needs of the specific plant species.

Fertilization: As the seedlings grow, provide them with a diluted liquid fertilizer formulated for young plants. Follow the package instructions for proper dilution ratios and frequency of application.

Transplanting Seedlings:

Harden Off Seedlings: Before transplanting seedlings into the garden, gradually expose them to outdoor conditions for 1 to 2 weeks.

Start with a few hours of outdoor exposure and gradually increase the duration each day. This process helps the seedlings acclimate to the outdoor environment.

Transplanting: Choose a suitable location in your garden with appropriate sunlight, soil, and spacing requirements for the specific plant species. Gently remove seedlings from their containers, taking care not to damage the roots. Dig a hole in the garden soil, place the seedling, and backfill with soil, firming it gently around the roots.

Watering and Care: Water the transplanted seedlings thoroughly after planting to settle the soil around the roots. Continue watering regularly until the seedlings establish themselves. Provide appropriate care, including watering, fertilizing, and protecting them from pests and diseases.

By following these steps, you can successfully propagate plants by seeds. Enjoy the journey of watching your seeds germinate, grow into seedlings, and eventually develop into mature plants that will beautify your garden or indoor spaces.

Common Mistakes to avoid

Common Mistakes to Avoid when Propagating Plants by Seeds:

1. **Overwatering:** One common mistake is overwatering the seeds or seedlings. Excessive moisture can lead to rotting or damping-off, a fungal disease that affects young seedlings. It's essential to maintain proper moisture levels by watering moderately and allowing the soil to partially dry out between waterings.

2. **Incorrect Sowing Depth**: Planting seeds at the wrong depth can impact germination rates and seedling development. Each plant species has specific requirements for sowing depth. Planting seeds too shallowly may result in poor germination while planting them too deeply can hinder their emergence. Follow the recommended sowing depth guidelines for each plant species.

3. **Insufficient Light:** Inadequate light can cause weak and leggy seedlings. Place the seed trays in a well-lit area or provide supplemental grow lights to ensure the seedlings receive sufficient light. Monitor the light intensity and duration to promote healthy growth.

4. **Lack of Patience**: It's important to remember that germination times can vary significantly among different plant species. Some seeds may take weeks or even months to germinate. Avoid the temptation to give up on slow-germinating seeds too soon.
Be patient and provide the optimal conditions required for each plant species.

5. **Poor Seed Quality**: Using low-quality or old seeds can result in low germination rates. It's crucial to obtain fresh, viable seeds from reputable sources. Perform a germination test on stored seeds or those collected from your garden to assess their viability before sowing.

6. **Lack of Labeling**: Failing to label your seed trays or pots can lead to confusion and difficulty in identifying the plant species as they grow. Label each container with the plant name, date of sowing, and any other relevant information. This will help you keep track of your plants and make adjustments if needed.

7. Inadequate Hardening Off Neglecting to harden off seedlings properly before transplanting them outdoors can result in transplant shock or stunted growth. Gradually expose the seedlings to outdoor conditions over some time to help them acclimate to the change in environment.

8. **Poor Pest and Disease Management:** Neglecting to monitor and address pests

and diseases can severely impact the success of your seedlings. Regularly inspect the plants for signs of pests or diseases and take appropriate measures, such as using organic pest control methods or applying suitable treatments, to mitigate any issues.

By avoiding these common mistakes, you can increase your chances of successful plant propagation by seeds and enjoy healthy, thriving seedlings that will eventually grow into beautiful plants.

Chapter 5: Propagation by Cuttings

Propagating plants by cuttings is a popular and effective method that allows you to reproduce plants with desirable traits. It's a way to create new plants that are genetically identical to the parent plant. Here's a step-by-step guide on how to propagate plants by cuttings:

Selecting and Preparing the Parent Plant:

- **Choose Healthy Parent Plant**: Select a healthy, mature plant with desirable characteristics for propagation. Ensure that the parent plant is free from diseases, pests, and any signs of stress.

- **Timing**: Determine the best time to take cuttings, as it can vary depending on the plant species and the type of cutting you're taking. Research or consult gardening references to determine the ideal timing for the specific plant you wish to propagate.

- **Tools**: Prepare sharp and clean pruning shears or a garden knife for taking cuttings. Sterilize the tools before use to prevent the spread of diseases.

Types of Cuttings

There are different types of cuttings you can take depending on the plant species and your desired propagation method:

- **Stem Cuttings**: Stem cuttings involve taking a section of the stem with a node or bud. This is the most common type of cutting used for propagation.

- **Leaf Cuttings**: Leaf cuttings involve removing a leaf or a portion of a leaf, including the petiole or stem. Some plants, such as African violets, can be propagated through leaf cuttings.

- **Root Cuttings**: Root cuttings involve taking a section of root with a bud or growth point. This method is typically used for plants with fleshy or woody roots.

- **Cane Cuttings**: Cane cuttings are specific to plants with long, flexible canes, such as roses or berries. A section of the cane is cut and prepared for propagation.

Taking and Preparing Cuttings:
- **Cutting Length**: Take cuttings that are 4 to 6 inches long, depending on the plant species. Ensure that each cutting has at least one node, which is a swollen area where leaves, buds, or roots emerge.

- **Remove Lower Leaves**: Trim away the lower leaves from the cutting, leaving only a few leaves at the top. This helps reduce water loss and prevents the cutting from wilting.

- **Auxin Application (Optional)**: Some plants benefit from the application of a rooting hormone or auxin to encourage root development. Follow the instructions on the rooting hormone package for proper application.

- **Remove Flowers or Buds**: If the parent plant has flowers or buds, it's advisable to remove them from the cuttings. This directs the plant's energy toward root development rather than flower production.

Rooting the Cuttings:

- **Rooting Medium**: Choose a suitable rooting medium based on the plant species. It could be a well-draining potting mix, vermiculite, perlite, or a specialized rooting medium. Moisten the medium before inserting the cuttings.

- **Inserting the Cuttings**: Make a hole or a slit in the rooting medium using a pencil or a dibber. Gently insert the prepared cuttings into the medium, ensuring that the lower nodes are in contact with the rooting medium.

- **Firming the Medium**: Gently firm the medium around the base of the cuttings to provide stability and good soil contact.

- **Moisture and Humidity**: Place the cuttings in a location with bright, indirect light. Maintain a high-humidity environment by covering the cuttings with a propagation dome, or plastic bag, or by using a misting system. This helps prevent excessive moisture loss and promotes root development.

Root Development and Transplanting:
- **Rooting Time**: Cuttings can take several weeks to months to develop roots. Monitor the cuttings regularly for signs of new growth or root development.

- **Transplanting**: Once the cuttings have developed a substantial root system, they are ready for transplanting. Carefully remove the cuttings from the rooting medium and transplant them into individual pots filled with a suitable potting mix.

- **Gradual Acclimatization:** Harden off the newly transplanted cuttings by gradually exposing them to outdoor conditions over some time. This helps them acclimate to the new environment and reduces transplant shock.

- **Post-Transplant Care:** Provide appropriate care, including watering, fertilizing, and protection from pests and diseases, to promote the healthy growth of the propagated plants.

By following these steps, you can successfully propagate plants by cutting them. Experiment with different plant species and cutting types to expand your garden and enjoy the satisfaction of growing new plants from existing ones.

Troubleshooting Common Issues in Propagation by Cuttings:

Rotting or Wilting Cuttings:

If your cuttings are rotting or wilting, it's usually a sign of excessive moisture or poor drainage. Check the rooting medium and ensure that it's well-draining. Avoid overwatering and allow the medium to partially dry out between waterings. If rotting occurs, remove the affected cuttings to prevent the spread of disease.

Lack of Root Development:

If your cuttings are not developing roots, it could be due to several factors:

- **Hormonal Imbalance**: Ensure that you've used a proper rooting hormone or auxin if required, and follow the instructions for application. Improper hormone concentration or application can hinder root development.

- **Improper Environmental Conditions:** Check the temperature and humidity levels. Some plants require specific environmental conditions for successful rooting. Adjust the conditions as needed to create an optimal rooting environment.

- **Inadequate Light**: Insufficient light can slow down or inhibit root development. Provide adequate bright, indirect light, or consider using supplemental grow lights to enhance rooting.

- **Poor Cutting Quality**: Ensure that you're using healthy, disease-free cuttings with viable nodes. Unhealthy or damaged cuttings may struggle to develop roots. Consider taking fresh cuttings from a healthy parent plant.

Fungal or Bacterial Diseases:

Cuttings are susceptible to fungal or bacterial diseases, especially in high-humidity environments. To prevent these issues:

- **Ensure Proper Sanitation**: Sterilize your tools and containers before use to prevent the introduction of pathogens. Use a clean, sterile rooting medium to reduce the risk of disease.

- **Provide Adequate Air Circulation:** Proper ventilation helps prevent the buildup of excess moisture and reduces the risk of fungal or bacterial infections. Avoid overcrowding the cuttings and provide enough space for air circulation.

- **Remove Affected Cuttings:** If you notice signs of disease on any cuttings, promptly remove and discard them to prevent the spread of infection to healthy cuttings.

Wilting or Drooping Leaves:

If the leaves on your cuttings are wilting or drooping, it could be a result of excessive moisture loss or inadequate water uptake. Check the moisture level of the rooting medium and adjust the watering accordingly. Mist the leaves or use a humidity dome to increase humidity around the cuttings.

Pest Infestation:

Cuttings can be vulnerable to pests such as aphids, mealybugs, or spider mites. If you notice signs of pest infestation, such as small insects, webbing, or distorted leaves, take immediate action to control the pests. Use appropriate organic or chemical treatments to eliminate the pests and prevent further damage.

Transplant Shock:

When transplanting rooted cuttings into individual pots or the garden, they may experience transplant shock. To minimize this:

- **Handle Cuttings Carefully:** Avoid damaging the roots or delicate new growth during the transplanting process.

- **Provide Adequate Water**: Water the transplanted cuttings immediately after transplanting to help them establish themselves in their new environment. Monitor soil moisture levels and water as needed until the plants have adjusted.

- **Gradual Acclimatization**: Harden off the transplanted cuttings gradually by exposing them to outdoor conditions over some time. This helps them adapt to the changes in light, temperature, and humidity.

By troubleshooting these common issues and making the necessary adjustments, you can increase your chances of successful plant propagation by cuttings and enjoy a thriving collection of propagated plants.

Propagating plant for beginners|52

Chapter 6: Propagation by Division

Propagation by division is a method commonly used for perennial plants that naturally produce multiple crowns or clumps. It involves separating these divisions from the parent plant to create new, independent plants. Here's a step-by-step guide on how to propagate plants by division:

Selecting and Preparing the Parent Plant:

- **Choose Healthy Parent Plant:** Select a healthy, mature plant with multiple crowns or clumps that are suitable for division. Ensure that the parent plant is free from diseases, pests, and any signs of stress.

- **Timing**: Determine the best time to divide the plant, as it can vary depending on the plant species and its growth cycle. Research or consult gardening references to find the ideal timing for the specific plant you wish to propagate.

- **Tools**: Prepare sharp and clean gardening tools, such as a garden fork, shovel, or pruning shears, for dividing the plant. Sterilize the tools before use to prevent the spread of diseases.

Dividing the Plant:
- **Watering**: Water the parent plant thoroughly for a day or two before dividing. This helps to ensure the plant is adequately hydrated, making it easier to separate the divisions.

- **Digging**: Carefully dig around the base of the parent plant, taking care not to damage the roots or the divisions. Use a garden fork or shovel to gently lift the clump out of the ground.

Division Methods:

- **Hand Division**: For plants with easily separable crowns or clumps, you can often separate them by hand. Gently pull or tease apart the divisions, ensuring that each division has sufficient roots and shoots.

- **Tool-Assisted Division:** Some plants may have dense or tightly intertwined root systems. In such cases, you may need to use gardening tools to divide the plant. Use a clean and sharp tool to cut through the root mass and separate the divisions.

Trim and Remove:

Trim any damaged or diseased portions from the divisions. Remove excess foliage or long roots, as this can help reduce stress on the plants during the division process.

Replanting the Divisions:

- **Soil Preparation:** Prepare the planting area by loosening the soil and removing any weeds or debris. Amend the soil with organic matter if needed, to improve drainage and fertility.

- **Planting Depth**: Dig individual holes for each division, ensuring that the planting depth matches the original depth of the parent plant. Place the divisions in the holes, spreading out the roots evenly.

- **Backfilling**: Fill the holes with soil, gently firming them around the roots to eliminate air pockets. Avoid compacting the soil excessively, as this can hinder root growth.

- **Watering and Mulching**: Water the newly planted divisions thoroughly to settle the soil around the roots. Apply a layer of organic mulch around the plants to help retain moisture and suppress weed growth.

- **Post-Planting Care**: Provide regular watering, appropriate fertilization, and protection from pests and diseases to promote the healthy establishment of the divided plants.

By following these steps, you can successfully propagate plants by division. Experiment with different plant species and observe how division can help expand your garden and create new plants with ease.

Tips for Successful Division in Plant Propagation:

- **Choose the Right Time**: Divide plants during their active growth phase or at specific times recommended for the particular plant species. This ensures that the divisions have the best chance of establishing and growing successfully.

- **Healthy Parent Plants**: Select parent plants that are healthy, vigorous, and free from diseases or pests. Healthy plants will have a higher chance of producing strong and viable divisions.

- **Prepare the Soil**: Before dividing, prepare the planting area by ensuring the soil is well-drained and rich in organic matter. This promotes healthy root development and overall plant growth.

- **Watering Before Division:** Water the parent plant thoroughly a day or two before dividing. Moist soil makes it easier to separate the divisions without causing excessive stress to the plants.

- **Divide with Care:** When dividing the plant, handle the divisions gently to avoid damaging the roots or the shoots. Use sharp and clean tools to make clean cuts or separate clumps by hand, ensuring that each division has sufficient roots and shoots.

- **Trim and Remove:** Trim any damaged or diseased portions from the divisions before replanting. Removing excess foliage or long roots can help reduce stress on the plants during the division process.

- **Plant Immediately**: Plant the divisions as soon as possible after separating them from the parent plant. This reduces the risk of damage to the delicate roots and ensures a higher success rate.

- **Adequate Spacing**: Provide enough space between divisions when replanting to allow for their future growth. Crowding can lead to competition for resources and hinder their overall development.

- **Watering and Mulching**: After replanting, water the divisions thoroughly to help settle the soil around the roots. Apply a layer of organic mulch around the plants to conserve moisture, suppress weeds, and provide insulation.

- **Monitor and Maintain:** Regularly monitor the newly divided plants for signs of stress, such as wilting or yellowing leaves. Provide appropriate care, including watering, fertilizing, and protection from pests and diseases, to ensure their successful establishment.

- **Gradual Transplantation:** If you are transplanting divisions into a new location, consider gradually acclimating them to their new environment. Start by placing them in a shaded or protected area and gradually exposing them to increasing levels of sunlight over some time.

- **Labeling**: Keep track of the different divisions by labeling them with the plant name and any relevant information. This helps you identify and care for each division appropriately.

By following these tips, you can increase your chances of successful division and enjoy the benefits of propagating new plants from existing ones.

Chapter 7: Propagation by Layering

Propagation by layering is a method that allows you to create new plants from the stems or branches of the parent plant while they are still attached. This technique encourages the development of roots on the stem or branch, and once the roots are established, the new plant can be separated from the parent plant. Here's a step-by-step guide on how to propagate plants by layering:

Selecting and Preparing the Parent Plant;

- **Choose Suitable Plants**: Select plants that have flexible, low-lying branches or stems that can be easily bent and buried in the soil. Not all plant species are suitable for layering, so research or consult gardening references to identify plants that respond well to this propagation method.

- **Timing**: Determine the best time to perform layering, as it can vary depending on the plant species and its growth cycle. Research or consult gardening references to find the ideal timing for the specific plant you wish to propagate.

- **Tools**: Prepare clean and sharp pruning shears or a garden knife for making necessary cuts. Sterilize the tools before use to prevent the spread of diseases.

Types of Layering

There are several methods of layering, and the appropriate method depends on the plant species and its growth habits. Here are three common types of layering:

- **Simple Layering**: In simple layering, a low-lying branch or stem is bent down and partially buried in the soil. Roots develop at the point of contact with the soil, and once established, the new plant can be separated.

- **Air Layering**: Air layering is used for plants that are difficult to propagate through other methods. In this method, a portion of the stem is girdled, and a rooting medium is applied around the girdled section. Roots develop in the moist rooting medium, and the rooted portion can be removed and potted as a new plant.

- **Tip Layering:** Tip layering involves burying the tip of a flexible branch or stem in the soil while keeping the rest of the plant above ground. Roots develop at the buried tip, and once rooted, they can be separated from the parent plant.

Performing Layering:
- **Selecting the Stem/Branch**: Choose a healthy, non-flowering stem or branch that is flexible and suitable for the chosen layering method. It should have a node or area where leaves emerge.

- **Wounding the Stem/Branch**: Create a small wound on the stem or branch by making a shallow cut or scratching the surface. This helps stimulate root development.

- **Burying the Stem/Branch**: For simple layering, bury the wounded section of the stem or branch in a prepared trench or hole. For air layering, apply a rooting medium (such as sphagnum moss or perlite) around the wounded section and wrap it with plastic or a rooting container.

- **Securing the Layered Section**: Secure the buried or wrapped section in place using stakes, rocks, or soil to prevent it from lifting or moving during the rooting process.

- **Providing Adequate Care**: Water the layered section regularly to keep the soil or rooting medium consistently moist. Monitor the progress and adjust watering as needed. Provide appropriate light conditions based on the plant's requirements.

Root Development and Separation

- **Rooting Time**: Roots can take several weeks to months to develop, depending on the plant species and layering method. Monitor the layered section regularly for signs of root growth.

- **Separating the New Plant**: Once roots have developed sufficiently, the layered section can be separated from the parent plant. Carefully dig around the rooted section, ensuring that the new plant has an adequate root system.

- **Potting or Transplanting**: Transfer the newly separated plant into a suitable pot or prepared planting area. Ensure the planting medium matches the plant's requirements. Water the newly potted or transplanted plant thoroughly to help it establish.

- **Post-Propagation Care:** Provide appropriate care to the new plant, including watering, fertilizing, and protection from pests and diseases. Gradually acclimate the new plant to its growing environment, especially if moving it outdoors.

Propagation by layering can be a rewarding method to create new plants that are genetically identical to the parent plant. By following these steps and selecting the right plants, you can successfully propagate plants through layering and expand your garden with healthy and thriving specimens.

Chapter 8: Care and Maintenance of Propagated Plants

Once you have successfully propagated your plants, it's important to provide them with proper care and maintenance to ensure their healthy growth and development. Here are some guidelines to follow:

Transplanting and Potting Up:
- When the propagated plants have developed a strong root system,

transplant them into individual pots or a suitable growing medium.
- Use a well-draining potting mix that is appropriate for the specific plant species.
- Handle the plants gently to avoid damaging the roots during the transplanting process.
- Ensure the new pots have adequate drainage holes to prevent waterlogging.

Watering and Fertilization:

- Water the propagated plants regularly, but avoid overwatering, as it can lead to root rot.
- Check the moisture level of the soil before watering by sticking your finger into the soil about an inch deep.
- Provide enough water to moisten the root zone thoroughly, but allow the soil to dry slightly between waterings.

- Fertilize the propagated plants with a balanced, water-soluble fertilizer according to the specific plant's requirements.
- Follow the manufacturer's instructions for dosage and frequency of application.
- Avoid over-fertilizing, as it can cause nutrient burn and harm the plants.

Providing Optimal Light Conditions:
- Place the propagated plants in an appropriate location with suitable light conditions.
- Most plants require bright, indirect light for healthy growth.
- Observe the specific light requirements of the propagated plants and position them accordingly.
- Some plants may require more direct sunlight, while others prefer partial shade.

Protection from Pests and Diseases:
- Regularly inspect the propagated plants for any signs of pests or diseases.
- Common pests include aphids, mealybugs, spider mites, and scale insects.
- Treat pest infestations promptly using organic or chemical insecticides, depending on your preference.
- If diseases are detected, such as fungal infections or leaf spots, take appropriate measures like removing infected parts and applying fungicides if necessary.
- Quarantine newly propagated plants to prevent the spread of pests or diseases to other plants.

Pruning and Maintenance:
- Regularly monitor the growth of the propagated plants and trim or prune as needed.

- Remove any dead or yellowing leaves to maintain plant health and appearance.
- Pinch back the tips of the plants to encourage bushier growth and prevent legginess.
- Monitor the size of the pots and repot the plants into larger containers when they outgrow their current ones.

Remember to research the specific care requirements of the propagated plant species you are working with, as different plants may have specific needs. By providing proper care, you can enjoy the growth and beauty of your propagated plants for years to come.

Chapter 9: Troubleshooting Common Issues with Propagated Plants

While propagating plants can be a rewarding experience, it's common to encounter certain issues along the way. Here are some common problems that may arise during plant propagation and suggestions for troubleshooting:

Rooting Failure:
- Ensure that the rooting medium or soil is well-draining and provides adequate moisture retention.
- Check the temperature and humidity levels, as extreme conditions can hinder root development.

- Use rooting hormones or growth enhancers to promote root growth.
- Consider adjusting the timing of propagation to a more suitable season for the specific plant species.
- Evaluate the health and quality of the parent plant from which the cuttings were taken.

Disease and Pest Infestations:
- Inspect the propagated plants regularly for signs of pests such as aphids, mealybugs, or spider mites.
- Remove any visible pests manually or use organic or chemical insecticides if necessary.
- Prevent disease spread by avoiding excessive moisture or overcrowding among the plants.
- If fungal or bacterial diseases are present, remove infected plant parts and

apply appropriate fungicides or bactericides.
- Maintain good hygiene practices by cleaning and sterilizing tools and containers to prevent the spread of pathogens.

Nutrient Deficiencies:
- Monitor the appearance of the propagated plants for signs of nutrient deficiencies, such as yellowing leaves or stunted growth.
- Adjust the pH of the soil or growing medium to ensure optimal nutrient availability.
- Use balanced fertilizers or specialized formulations to address specific nutrient deficiencies.
- Follow the recommended dosage and frequency of fertilizer application, as

over-fertilizing can lead to nutrient toxicity.

Environmental Stress:
- Evaluate the growing conditions of the propagated plants, including light, temperature, and humidity levels.
- Adjust the light intensity or duration to match the plant's requirements.
- Ensure proper ventilation to prevent excessive humidity or stagnant air.
- Protect the plants from extreme temperatures, drafts, or sudden temperature fluctuations.
- Avoid placing the propagated plants in direct sunlight if they require shade or partial shade.

Improper Watering:
- Determine the water requirements of the propagated plants and avoid overwatering or underwatering.
- Check the moisture level of the soil regularly and water when the top inch of the soil feels dry.
- Use the appropriate watering method, such as bottom watering or misting, based on the plant's needs.
- Adjust the frequency and amount of watering according to environmental conditions and plant growth stage.

Transplant Shock:
- Gradually acclimate the propagated plants to new growing conditions if they are being transplanted to a different environment.

- Minimize root disturbance during transplanting and handle the plants gently.
- Provide extra care and attention to the transplanted plants by ensuring adequate moisture, humidity, and protection from direct sunlight.

Remember that troubleshooting can be a process of trial and error. It's important to observe and learn from the issues you encounter while propagating plants, adjusting your techniques and care practices accordingly. By addressing problems promptly, you can increase the success rate and overall health of your propagated plants.

Chapter 10: Propagating Specific Plant Species

Different plant species may have specific requirements and techniques for successful propagation. Here are some guidelines for propagating specific plant species commonly encountered by beginners:

Herbs and Vegetables:

- Many herbs and vegetables can be propagated through stem cuttings. Take 4-6 inch cuttings from healthy, non-flowering stems and remove the lower leaves before planting in a well-draining medium.

- Some herbaceous plants, like basil or mint, can also be propagated from leaf cuttings by selecting healthy leaves and placing them in water or a rooting medium until roots develop.

- Certain vegetables, such as tomatoes or peppers, can be propagated through seeds. Collect ripe fruits, extract the seeds, and sow them in a seed-starting mix.

Ornamental Plants:

- Many ornamental plants, such as roses, hydrangeas, or azaleas, can be propagated through stem cuttings. Choose healthy, semi-hardwood, or hardwood stems, remove any flowers or buds, and treat the cuttings with a rooting hormone before planting.

- Some ornamental plants, like African violets or succulents, can be propagated from leaf cuttings. Gently remove a healthy leaf and place it in a moist, well-draining medium until roots develop.

- Some ornamental grasses and ferns can be propagated through division. Carefully separate the root mass into smaller sections, ensuring each division has healthy roots and shoots.

Succulents and Cacti:

- Succulents and cacti can often be propagated from stem or leaf cuttings. Allow the cuttings to dry for a few days to form calluses before planting in a well-draining succulent or cactus mix.

- Some succulents, like jade plants, can also be propagated through leaf propagation. Gently remove a healthy leaf and place it on top of well-draining soil, keeping it slightly moist until new plantlets emerge.

Houseplants:

- Many common houseplants, such as pothos, philodendrons, or snake plants, can be propagated through stem cuttings. Take 4-6 inch cuttings with several nodes and plant them in a moist, well-draining medium.

- Some houseplants, like spider plants or aloe vera, can be propagated through plantlets or offsets. Carefully detach the plantlets or offsets from the parent plant and plant them in their containers.

Fruit Trees and Shrubs:

- Some fruit trees and shrubs can be propagated through hardwood or softwood cuttings, such as apple trees or blueberry bushes. Take 6-8 inch cuttings, remove any flowers or buds, and follow specific guidelines for each plant species.

- Fruit trees can also be propagated through grafting techniques, such as budding or whip-and-tongue grafting. These techniques require more skill and knowledge, so it's advisable to learn from experienced gardeners or horticulturists.

Remember to research the specific propagation techniques and requirements for the plant species you are working with. Understanding the ideal time, method, and conditions for propagation will greatly increase your chances of success. With practice and experience, you can master the art of propagating various plant species and expand your gardening skills.

Chapter 11: Taking Your Propagation Skills Further

Once you have mastered the basics of plant propagation, there are several ways you can further develop your skills and expand your knowledge in this area. Here are some suggestions for taking your propagation skills to the next level:

Experimenting with Hybridization:
- Explore the fascinating world of hybridization by crossing different plant varieties within the same species.
- Learn about the principles of pollination and how to control the transfer of pollen between plants.
- Document and observe the results of your hybridization experiments to discover new and unique plant combinations.

Creating New Varieties:
- Use your knowledge of plant genetics and propagation techniques to develop new plant varieties with desirable traits.
- Select parent plants with distinct characteristics and cross-pollinate them to create offspring with unique traits.
- Observe and evaluate the traits of the resulting plants, selecting and propagating those that display the desired qualities.

Participating in Plant Swaps and Exchanges:
- Engage with other gardeners and plant enthusiasts by participating in plant swaps or exchanges.

- Share your propagated plants with others and acquire new varieties in return.
- Attend local gardening events, and plant fairs, or join online gardening communities to connect with fellow plant enthusiasts and expand your plant collection.

Continuing Education:
- Take courses or workshops on plant propagation offered by botanical gardens, universities, or horticultural societies.
- Attend seminars or lectures by experienced propagators to learn advanced techniques and gain valuable insights.
- Read books, articles, and scientific publications on plant propagation to deepen your understanding of the subject.

Documenting and Recording:
- Keep a detailed record of your propagation endeavors, noting the techniques, materials, and observations for each plant species.
- Take photographs or create a plant propagation journal to document the progress of your propagated plants over time.
- Use these records to track your successes, learn from your failures, and refine your propagation techniques.

Volunteer or Work in a Horticultural Setting:
- Seek opportunities to volunteer at botanical gardens, nurseries, or horticultural centers to gain practical experience and learn from experts in the field.

- Consider pursuing a career in horticulture or becoming a professional propagator to further develop your skills and knowledge.

Remember, developing your propagation skills is an ongoing process that requires patience, experimentation, and continuous learning. Each new plant you propagate presents a unique opportunity to expand your knowledge and contribute to the world of gardening and horticulture. Enjoy the journey and never stop exploring the wonders of plant propagation.

Chapter 12: Advanced Tips and Techniques for Plant Propagation

Tissue Culture:

Tissue culture is an advanced propagation technique that involves growing plants from small plant tissue samples in a controlled laboratory environment. It allows for the rapid production of a large number of identical plants and is commonly used for rare or difficult-to-propagate species.

Grafting and Budding:

Grafting and budding are techniques used to combine the desirable qualities of two different plant varieties into a single plant. These methods are particularly useful for fruit trees, roses, and ornamental plants. Grafting involves joining a stem (scion) of one plant onto the root system (rootstock) of another while budding involves inserting a bud from one plant into another.

Micropropagation:

Micropropagation, also known as in vitro propagation, involves growing plants in a sterile laboratory environment using tissue culture techniques. This method allows for the production of a large number of disease-free and genetically identical plants from a small plant sample.

Air Pruning:

Air pruning is a technique used to promote healthy root development in container-grown plants. By using containers with air-permeable walls or adding air pruning pots, the roots are exposed to air, which causes them to dry out and encourages the growth of lateral roots. This helps prevent root circling and promotes a more fibrous root system.

Bottom Heat:

Providing bottom heat to rooting media can stimulate root growth and enhance the success of propagation. Using a propagation heat mat or heating cables under the containers or propagating trays can create a warm environment that encourages faster and more vigorous root development.

Scarification:

Scarification involves breaking or weakening the seed coat to facilitate germination. Some hard-coated seeds may have dormancy mechanisms that require scarification to allow moisture and oxygen to penetrate the seed for germination. Scarification methods include soaking in hot water, rubbing seeds on abrasive surfaces, or nicking the seed coat.

Stratification:

Stratification is a technique used to simulate the natural winter dormancy requirements of certain seeds. It involves subjecting seeds to a period of cold, moist conditions to break seed dormancy and promote germination. This can be done by refrigerating seeds in a moist medium for a specific duration before sowing.

Rooting Hormone Alternatives:

While synthetic rooting hormones are commonly used in plant propagation, some natural alternatives can stimulate root growth as well. Willow water, made by soaking willow branches in water, contains natural rooting hormones that can be used as a rooting hormone substitute for certain plants.

Hybridization:

Hybridization involves cross breeding two different plant varieties or species to create new plants with desirable characteristics. This advanced technique requires knowledge of plant genetics and pollination methods to successfully create and propagate hybrid plants.

Controlled Environment Propagation:
Creating a controlled environment, such as a greenhouse or indoor grow room, allows for precise control of temperature, humidity, light, and other environmental factors. This level of control enhances the success of propagation, especially for plants with specific requirements or those propagated during unfavorable seasons.

Remember that advanced propagation techniques may require specialized knowledge, equipment, and experience. It's important to thoroughly research and understand the specific requirements and techniques associated with each method before attempting them.

Conclusion

Plant propagation is an exciting and rewarding practice that allows you to expand your garden, create new plants, and explore the wonders of plant reproduction. Whether you are a beginner or have some experience, understanding the different methods and techniques of plant propagation can greatly enhance your gardening skills.

In this comprehensive guide, we have covered the essential aspects of plant propagation for beginners, including an introduction to plant propagation, and understanding different propagation methods such as propagation by seeds, cuttings, division, and layering. We also explored the necessary tools and maintenance for successful propagation.

Additionally, we discussed common mistakes to avoid and troubleshooting tips for common propagation problems, ensuring that you are well-prepared to overcome challenges that may arise during the propagation process.

For those seeking more advanced techniques, we provided insights into tissue culture, grafting, micropropagation, and other specialized methods that can take your propagation skills to the next level.

Remember, successful plant propagation requires patience, attention to detail, and a bit of experimentation. Each plant species may have its unique requirements and preferences, so it's important to research and understand the specific needs of the plants you are propagating.

By mastering the art of plant propagation, you can multiply your favorite plants, share them with friends and family, and create a beautiful and diverse garden that reflects your passion for plants.

So, roll up your sleeves, gather your tools, and embark on your plant propagation journey. Enjoy the process of nurturing new life, watching roots develop, and witnessing the growth and beauty of the plants you propagate. Happy propagating!